DEVON TRACTION

Stephen Heginbotham

AMBERLEY

This book is dedicated to friends old and new.

First published 2020

Amberley Publishing
The Hill, Stroud
Gloucestershire, GL5 4EP

www.amberley-books.com

Copyright © Stephen Heginbotham, 2020

The right of Stephen Heginbotham to be identified
as the Author of this work has been asserted
in accordance with the Copyright, Designs and
Patents Act 1988.

ISBN 978 1 4456 8019 4 (print)
ISBN 978 1 4456 8020 0 (ebook)

British Library Cataloguing in Publication Data.
A catalogue record for this book is available from
the British Library.

Typesetting by Aura Technology and Software
Services, India. Printed in the UK.

Introduction

This book has been compiled using sets of photographs taken over several decades throughout Devon and depicts the many and varied traction types and trains that were once a familiar sight every day on the rails of this Riviera county. Most are previously unpublished.

Devon is generally associated with holiday trains, particularly those serving idyllic locations such as Torquay and Barnstaple, but it is sometimes forgotten that large amounts of freight passed through, to and from Cornwall, as well as freight generated within Devon. Postal, Parcels, Newspapers, Perishables, Fish trains and much more were all scheduled within this picturesque and popular holiday county.

Though such political short-sightedness has ostensibly disappeared in the main, there still remains a fragmented network driven by targets and subsidies. The political dream of previous governments that they could generate competition and improve things has not happened, even though the various managements and politicians would have you believe otherwise.

As the semaphore signals disappeared throughout the county, a new modern panel signalbox was opened in Exeter working alongside three traditional signalboxes, though they were all modernised with mini-panels. The panel signalbox in Plymouth was already well established by the time Exeter Panel opened, but aside from boxes along the former Southern Line to Waterloo, little else remained of the former network of lines once reaching every corner of the county.

The redoubtable Dr Richard Beeching and his report 'The Reshaping of British Railways' was not the magic pill it was conceived as all those years ago. Basically, he was an accountant and lacked the vision and foresight of the great innovators, engineers and pioneers that built the railways. Of course, nowadays he is reviled by many for destroying the network and for leaving many large and small communities without a decent public transport service. A good example is Tavistock, in West Devon, which is now trying to restore a rail link to Plymouth.

Many arguments about the Dawlish route have rumbled on for years, and it was certainly not the best of ideas to leave the West Country with just one extremely vulnerable route into the far west.

As mentioned above, Devon, like many other rural areas, suffered at the hands of Dr Beeching and also from intransigent managements, but did manage to keep hold of some of its beautiful branch lines to the coast and country.

This excellent set of photographs has been provided from the collections of some good friends and former colleagues of mine, as well as some of my own.

Like Cornwall, Devon has had a varied history of diesel traction types over the last six decades, after steam started to disappear in the 1960s and like all things 'Great Western', the Western Region of British Railways was different when it came to diesel traction and, along with the former LSWR and later Southern lines, a true variety could be encountered around Exeter, it being the central hub of the Devon network.

The main route out of London Paddington to the West Country and the ultimate destination of Penzance was once the domain of the diesel hydraulics, such as the famous Westerns, or Warships. Like GWR, it wanted to promote its region by giving its frontline locomotives names that reflected both the region and its close association with the sea. These names meant something; they promoted the railway and gave a sense of pride amongst the staff and people travelling along the Western Region routes.

The diesel hydraulics were, of course, non-standard in British Railways terms and as time went on it became apparent that these wonderful locomotives were on notice. As they came up for heavy overhaul, or as they failed, more and more were sidelined in favour of more standard locos, such as the ubiquitous Class 47s.

As the West Coast electrification was completed from London to Scotland the English Electric locomotives that had been used north of Crewe became surplus and were cascaded to the Western Region. So now the famous fifty 50s started to replace the Westerns. The Western Region, of course, put their mark on them and they took the names of previously withdrawn locomotives, predominately with naval connections.

By summer 1976 all fifty had been transferred, but the failure rate was high and down to 50 per cent at times, so they were progressively rebuilt/refurbished in the early 1980s. Though failures continued, reliability was much improved. By February 1987 spares were becoming scarce and BR seriously considered scrapping them all, but a traction shortage of suitable motive power prevented this. Consequently, 50011 was withdrawn as a source of spares and double-heading used where possible to improve performance. More spares were needed so in July 1987 50006 was withdrawn, followed by 50014 in December. The 50s also found fame in their twilight years operating along the former LSWR route to London Waterloo from Exeter St David's alongside many other types of traction.

As we came through to the 1990s the 50s slowly gave way to the HSTs and 159s, and the Class 46s gave way to the 37s, the Class 66s eventually arriving for freight haulage. The Voyagers replaced the HSTs and Class 47s on cross-country workings and, whilst they are fast, they are noisy and uncomfortable in standard class. They are, after all, just a DMU! Soon we will see the next generation of passenger train to replace the HST, which is, arguably, Britain's most successful train. As the modern railway tries to drag itself into the twenty-first century, we will soon see these new high-speed DMUs dominate the tracks and, aside from infrequent freight duties and occasional specials, the railways of the UK will be, in my opinion, a boring, corporate place for the true enthusiast.

One thing is certain though: we will never see the likes of a Western, Warship, 37, 45, or 50 thrashing through Devon again, apart from the odd preserved example on a special.

I hope this collection of excellent photographs stirs memories of happier times on the tracks of the Riviera County. Whilst most images are of excellent quality, a few are not as good as one would have liked but are included for their general interest and historical importance. Also included in this final year of traditional (GWR) HST operations in the West Country is a photographic tribute to these wonderful trains, with pictures taken in the final weeks and days leading up to the final day on 18 May 2019. Enjoy!

In the year that saw the traditional Great Western HST train bow out of normal use in the West Country, I thought it fitting to start this collection of photographs with an image (not top quality) of 253016 (43032 or 33) leaving the Royal Albert Bridge and entering Devon. The picture detail suggests it is the first HST to have done so, which would mean it was *c.* 1979. However, the InterCity 'executive' grey and yellow suggests it was the early 1980s. (Author's Collection)

An unidentified pair of Class 31s hammers through Dawlish Warren with an Up train in Semaphore signalling days, *c.* 1982. The camping coaches are synonymous with Dawlish Warren and the connection to the goods yard appears to still be in place. (Author's Collection)

On the Down through line at Dawlish Warren on Saturday 13 August 1977, we see Class 47014 with the 08.40 Liverpool to Paignton, consisting of twelve Mk 1 coaches. Built as D1543 in October 1963, and withdrawn in May 1990, it was scrapped in April 1992. (Author's Collection [original - R. Greaves])

A Down mixed freight passes through Dawlish Warren *c.* 1989 with grey, large-logo 47337 (D1818) *Herbert Austin* in charge. The loco went on to be rebuilt as 57602 *Restormel Castle* from November 2003 and survives today. (Author's Collection)

Exeter St David's Station in 1991 sees Network SouthEast-liveried 50018 *Resolution* about to depart for London Waterloo. It was withdrawn in July of the same year and scrapped in January 1993 by M. C. Processors of Glasgow. (Author's Collection)

On an unspecified date in June 1973, a split-four-character route indicator Class 45 traverses the sea wall with a Down cross-country train. (Author's Collection)

Paignton Station *c*. 1988 and an unidentified Class 50 waits for the semaphore signal (11) to clear for the Up departure. (Author's Collection)

'Peak' number 45016 (D16) is seen here traversing the extremely scenic line along the sea wall and through Dawlish with an unspecified Up train in the 1970s or 1980s. The loco was cut up in October 1986 by Vic Berry, Leicester. (Author's Collection)

Class 52 (D)1045 *Western Viscount* at Newton Abbot on 20 March 1974. 1B15 was the 10.30 Paddington–Penzance (Cornish Riviera) at that time. Built at Crewe in November 1962, it was withdrawn just twelve years later and scrapped in August 1975 at Swindon. (Paul Webber Collection)

English Electric 37156 and 37111 and an Exeter Riverside to Exmouth Junction Stone Working at Exmouth Junction on 25 February 1998. 37156 (D6856) was built in July 1963, withdrawn in June 1999 and scrapped by EWS (CDRC) at Wigan in January 2000. 37111 (D6811) was built in February 1963 and withdrawn just six months after this picture, being broken up for spares by HNRC in July 2003. (Graham Bowden)

Leaving Exeter St David's on Saturday 27 May 1978, and about to tackle the 1:37 gradient up to Exeter Central and onwards along the Southern Route towards Salisbury and London Waterloo, is a pair of Birmingham Railway Carriage & Wagon-built (BRC&W) Class 33s: 33064 (D6584) and 33035 (D6553). The former was built in January 1962, withdrawn in October 1994 and scrapped in July 1997 by M. R. J. Phillips, and the latter was built in May 1961 and withdrawn in September 1996, surviving in preservation. (Maurice Dart)

Crediton on Saturday 2 May 1988 and 47340 (D1821), with the Chipman's Weedkilling Train, is seen returning from a trip to Okehampton. The March 1965 Brush-built loco was withdrawn in June 1998 and scrapped at Crewe in January 1999. (Graham Bowden)

Brush Class 31 31415 (D5824) is seen stored along with several other locos at Meldon on Sunday 8 May 2005. It was to be another four years before it was cut up by Booths of Rotherham. (Maurice Dart)

Hauling a WCML DVT, set up through Aller on Saturday 7 September 1991, is 47338 (D1819). I had spent part of the afternoon on the bridge and according to my notes the 47 had headed down the branch at 15.48. Presumably this had been on standby at Newton Abbot. This job was routinely covered by a Speedlink 47 from Exeter stabling point. This February 1965 Brush-built loco was withdrawn in April 1999 and scrapped by Booths in July 2007. (Paul Webber)

Dual fuel (600 hp diesel and 750v third-rail) Class 73 73134 (D6041) is seen here at Okehampton in use on the Dartmoor Railway on an unknown date. The English Electric loco was built in August 1966 and withdrawn in April 1999, surviving in private preservation but not on the Dartmoor Railway. (Late Jim Renshaw – Author's Collection)

Network SouthEast-liveried English Electric 50044 (D444) *Exeter* is seen here in its namesake city with a train of Mk 2 matching liveried coaches, having likely arrived off the Southern from Salisbury on an unknown date (*c.* 1990). Built in November 1968 and withdrawn in January 1991 from Laira, it was purchased for preservation by The Fifty Fund and is main line certified. (Author's Collection)

Passing along Dawlish Warren on Saturday 24 July 1999 is 1C05, the 07.00 Bristol Temple Meads to Paignton with 47840 (D1661/47077/47613). Built at Crewe in March 1965 and withdrawn in May 2007, it survives in preservation on the West Somerset Railway. (Graham Bowden)

A cracking photograph of 47593 *Galloway Princess* that could be from the 1980s but was taken at Exeter on 14 May 2019. This well-kept Direct Rail Services (DRS) loco was built by BR at Crewe in November 1965, and carried several numbers over the years (D1973/47272/47673/47790). 47593 is seen on the 09.40 Goodrington Sands–Barton Hill. (Martin Duff)

An unidentified Network SouthEast-liveried Class 50 sits in Platform 1 at Exeter St David's Station with a train for London Waterloo on an unknown date in the late 1980s. It is pulling a train of NSE-liveried coaches, except for one in blue and grey. (Author's Collection)

On Sunday 1 May 1994 a rail fair, opened by Pete Waterman, was held in Exeter Riverside Yard, and which I attended. It was one of the final gestures of British Rail, before the slow dissection of the big family started in earnest. Locos present were Class 45 D120, AC electrics 83012 and 85101, 47004, 59102, 31110, 50031, D212, 55015, D7017 and D821, amongst many others. (Author)

Also present at the rail fair were West Country Pacific loco Class 34105 *Swanage,* Merchant Navy Class 35005 *Canadian Pacific* and Warship Diesel Hydraulic D821 *Greyhound.* (Author's Collection)

Class 50 50008 *Thunderer* is seen here in charge of an engineering train on the Down line at Teignmouth in January 1989. The wagons are ZFV, Dogfish ballast hoppers. Number 8 survives, of course. (Author's Collection)

Dawlish on Monday 29 September 1986 and 50024 *Vanguard* is seen with a Down stopping service. Built in June 1968, it was withdrawn in February 1991 and scrapped five months later at Old Oak Common. (Graham Bowden)

On Saturday 27 May 1989, Class 31s 31437 and 31462 had struck out from New Street with 1V46, the 09.33 Stockport to Paignton. 437 was removed at Bristol, leaving 462 to carry on alone. This picture is at Sprey Point, Teignmouth, running around sixty minutes late but well on the way to Paignton. 462 did the return service to Wolverhampton solo, as this was a relatively light load. Neither loco survived but both were stored for several years before being cut up. (Paul Webber)

Plymouth Station, Saturday 19 July 2014, and 57604 *Pendennis Castle* is on Platform 7 with a short rake of Mk 3 day coaches, possibly off the Sleeper service and forming the afternoon Class 2 train from Penzance. (Maurice Dart)

Exeter St David's Station before the 159s took over the Waterloo trains. Here is Network SouthEast-liveried 50043 *Eagle* having arrived with a Down train. Withdrawn in February 1991 and initially set aside for preservation, it was cut up eleven years later. (Author's Collection)

In June 1973, we see a Down cross-country express along the sea wall, with an unidentified Class 45/46 in charge of what purports to be 1V82. Semaphore signalling still reigns supreme. (Author's Collection)

An interesting photograph, *c.* 1990, of five Class 50s in what appears to be Ocean Siding at Plymouth Laira Depot. They are possibly withdrawn and stored or are awaiting transfer for scrapping. 50020, 50021 and 50040 are all visible, along with two NSE-liveried examples. 50020 was cut up in June 1992, 50021 is preserved and 50040 was cut up only eleven years ago. (Author's Collection)

The 1987-built Track Assessment Unit was constructed by BREL at York after the Class 150/1 'Sprinter' units were completed. 950001 is seen on Tuesday 23 September 2014 at Plymouth in the west end bay (P2), adjacent to where the Gunnislake trains depart from. (Maurice Dart)

A pre-1987 photograph of Newton Abbot Station showing a grand array of semaphore signalling and Newton Abbot West signalbox. What appears to be a Class 50 is set to depart from the Up-Main platform in the Down direction, probably after bringing a train in from the west and terminating at Newton Abbot. (Author's Collection)

Here we see 50044 *Exeter* again, arriving into Exeter St David's Station with either a charter or service train off the Waterloo line, *c.* 1990. (Author's Collection)

Crediton on Thursday 7 May 1987 and we find 20901 and 20904 with the Chipman's Weedkilling Train returning from a trip to Barnstaple. 20901 (D8101/20101) was built by English Electric (EE) in November 1961 and later operated by Hunslet Barclay (HB). It was then sold to Direct Rail Services (DRS) in October 1998 and withdrawn in September 2003. It is currently shown as stored. 20904 (D8041/20041) was built by EE in November 1959 and, after being operated by HB, as seen here, and subsequently DRS in October 1998, it was withdrawn in March 2003 and is shown as stored at Long Marston. (Graham Bowden)

Exmouth Junction on Tuesday 31 March 1998 and 7W70 Chard Junction to Exeter Riverside is seen with 37197. The English Electric loco was built as D6897 at Robert Stephenson & Hawthorn Works in April 1964 and, after being withdrawn by EWS Railway in December 1999, it passed to DRS and subsequently to East Lancashire Railway and then to West Coast Railway (WCRC), where it is still in service. These versatile locomotives could be found almost anywhere on the network and on any type of train and were known affectionately as 'Tractors' by enthusiasts. (Graham Bowden)

'Peak' Class 45 45121 is seen on Saturday 7 August 1982 passing along the sea wall with a short Up parcels service. Built by BR at Derby in December 1960 as D18, it was withdrawn in November 1987 and scrapped in September 1993. (Author's Collection)

The 14.42 Exeter to Barnstaple train passing Barnstaple Inner Home signal with 31124 on Saturday 9 August 1986. This loco was built by Brush in July 1959 as D5542 but served for almost thirty-one years before finally being scrapped in November 1991. (Graham Bowden)

An unidentified Class 50 in NSE livery pulls out of Platform 3 at Exeter St David's Station and probably into the sidings to run round for the return journey to London Waterloo, *c.* 1990. (Author's Collection)

Seen at Crediton on Saturday 15 March 2003 is Class 52 'Western' D1015 *Western Champion* with an Okehampton to Crewe Railtour, 'The Western Quarryman'. In 2010 D1015 was used as part of the Great Western 175 celebrations and after taking a train to Penzance from Par, it returned to St Blazey. It was then tasked with taking the stock back to Penzance, on Monday 28 June, with steam locos Castle 5029 on the front and King 6024 on the rear in light steam. I was asked to act as Pilotman for the move over the Up line from Truro to Penzance at 03.00 hours due to clearance issues with the King on the Down line. A high point in my career, the departure from Truro with this magnificent machine was awe inspiring and must have awoken a few residents! (Graham Bowden)

The glory days in Devon. Not a sight we are ever likely to see again, apart from the occasional special. An unidentified Class 50 and a complete rake of Mk 1 coaches heads along the Up line through Dawlish in June 1981. (Author's Collection)

A Laira Open Day on Sunday 15 September 1991 and we see 50049 (D49) *Defiance* (minus nameplates), and 50018 (D18) *Resolution*. Both had been recently withdrawn. 50049 had been repainted trainload grey, renumbered (50149) and reclassified (with Class 37 bogies) as a freight loco from 1987 to 1989. It survives in preservation. 50018 was scrapped in January 1993. (Maurice Dart)

A photograph of a rare unit. AC Cars W79976 was one of only five built. It was introduced in 1958 for use on the Scottish and Western Regions and in Bodmin. This picture, taken on Saturday 24 April 1965, shows the unit at Newton Abbot Depot in company with D1064 *Western Regent*. Quite why this particular one is in Newton Abbot Depot at that time is not known as the two serving Bodmin North were normally 79977/8. 79975 and 79978 were used between Yeovil Town and Yeovil Junction until October 1966 and were transferred to Scotland in January 1967. (Maurice Dart)

On 25 July 1987, 31142 is seen at Crediton with the 17.26 Barnstaple to Exeter service. This loco dates from October 1959 and served for a little under forty years. It was not until December 2003 that it was finally cut up. (Graham Bowden)

A dull Friday at Dawlish in June 2001 and unique liveried 57601 pauses with the 09.20 Plymouth to Paddington. This product of Brush started life as a Class 47, D1759 in August 1964, then through other incarnations as 47165, 47590 and 47825. It was withdrawn in May 2000 and rebuilt as a Class 57 in April 2001. It still exists and is shown as WCRC. (Martin Duff)

Exeter St David's Station *c.* 1989 and an unidentified Class 50 (possibly 50029) awaits departure time with an early evening train for the southern route to Salisbury and Waterloo. (Author's Collection)

A classic Teignmouth photograph. A summer Saturday service passes beneath the Skew Bridge with the 08.58 from Paignton, on 23 June 2001, with a nicely turned out Virgin CrossCountry Class 47. (Martin Duff)

A picture of Derby-built Class 08 shunter loco D4010 (08842) at Plymouth Station. The loco dated from 1960, and the photo could have been taken *c.* 1962. It was renumbered in March 1974. (Author's Collection)

A portrait of Intercity-liveried 08 shunter 08644 *Ponsondane* inside Plymouth Laira Depot on 17 July 1988. This Horwich-built loco started life as D3811 in February 1959 and is still in use with First Great Western Trains at Laira. (Author's Collection)

Class 50 number 50002 *Superb* races along the sea wall on an unspecified date in the blue/grey period with a train of Mk 1 and 2 coaches. It was withdrawn in September 1991 but survives in preservation in Devon. It was the first of its class to haul a passenger train in preservation. (Author's Collection)

Another unidentified Class 50 with a train for the southern route on Platform 1 at Exeter St David's Station *c.* 1989. (Author's Collection)

Platform 3 at Exeter St David's Station and an evening picture of Network SouthEast-liveried 50029 *Renown*, having arrived off the southern route. It was built in July 1968 as D429 and was withdrawn from Laira after engine failure in March 1991. It survives in preservation and has been cosmetically restored. (Author's Collection)

A Fragonset Class 47 pauses at Torquay with a Liverpool to Paignton train of mixed livery Mk 2 stock in mid-summer 2001. (Martin Duff)

The 10.01 Paignton to Newcastle, 1E33, passes Rewe with Virgin CrossCountry 47711. Built in June 1966 as D1941 and renumbered to 47498, it was withdrawn in June 2000 and broken up by HNRC at Toton in September 2004. It was also involved in an accident at Yeovil on 21 September 1991, sustaining moderate front end damage, which was subsequently repaired. (Graham Bowden)

NSE-liveried 50017 *Royal Oak*, is set for departure from Exeter St David's Station and routed to the Down Main (DM) with a train for the west. Built as D417 in April 1968, it was withdrawn in September 1991 but survives in preservation, being main line certified until late 2018. It has recently been sold to the Great Central Railway (GCR). (Author's Collection)

Another picture of 50029 *Renown,* seen as darkness falls on Platform 3 at Exeter St David's Station *c.* 1990. (Author's Collection)

On Monday 17 July 1989, near Totnes, we see a triple-headed combination made up of 47591 (D1965), 50003 (D403) *Temeraire* and 50037 (D437) *Illustrious.* The reason for such a move is unknown, though it makes a great picture and shows two very popular liveries. It is interesting that in the month this picture was taken, 47591 was renumbered 47804 and received two further renumbers before passing to the WCRC. Both 50s were scrapped in 1992. Storming the charts was 'Ride on Time' by Black Box. (Author's Collection)

Another view of 50003 but this time at Laira on Sunday 17 July 1988, which is coincidentally exactly one year earlier. In the charts at No. 1 was Yazz and the Plastic Population with 'The Only Way is Up'. (Maurice Dart)

Class 47 47553 (D1956) sweeps around the curves of the sea wall towards Teignmouth on an unspecified date in the 1980s. Built in December 1966, it was withdrawn in 1995. It would be another twelve years before it was scrapped. (Author's Collection)

Exeter St David's Station on 25 August 1992 sees 47350 (D1831) with the 12.17 to London Waterloo. This freight sector loco was probably standing in for a Class 50. Unofficially named *Scorpion*, it was subsequently rebuilt in 1998 as Class 57 57005 *Freightliner Excellence* and survives as such. It previously carried the name *British Petroleum* from 1987 to 1990. (Author's Collection)

On 22 April 2005, near Bow on the Okehampton Line, is light engine 47150 (D1743) with 0Z48, the 14.31 Meldon Quarry to Kingsland Road route learning trip. This June 1964-built example was withdrawn in July 2007 and cut up December 2010. (Graham Bowden)

Exeter St David's Station and two unidentified NSE-liveried Class 50s can be seen, one of which is on a special train. (Author's Collection)

Another picture of 50044 (D444) arriving at Exeter St David's Station off the southern route from Exeter Central Station. (Author's Collection)

Another picture of 47150 with a Meldon-Kingsland Road route learner at Crediton on Friday 22 April 2005. (Graham Bowden)

Horse Cove and 47825 (D1759) *Thomas Telford* is seen with the 09.18 Manchester Piccadilly to Plymouth on Saturday 13 July 1991. It was rebuilt as 57601. (Author's Collection)

The ubiquitous 50029 *Renown* is seen again here on Platform 1 at Exeter St David's Station awaiting departure for Salisbury and Waterloo. (Author's Collection)

D6315 was built by North British in January 1960 and completed only eleven years in service before withdrawal one month after this picture was taken, where it is depicted as 'stored-unserviceable' at Laira Depot. It was scrapped in January 1972, and none of the fifty-eight of these diesel-hydraulics survived. Not a successful locomotive. It keeps company with Class 47s 1680 (47094 from April 1974) and 1806 (47325 from March 1974) on Wednesday 7 April 1971. (Maurice Dart)

Class 58s were not that common in Devon but here is 58002 *Daw Mill Colliery* on 6V62, the Fawley to Tavistock Junction working, on 9 August 1999. It is seen here plunging into the gloom by Marine Parade at 19.18. It was still carrying 1Z58 'The Worksop Aberdonian' lettering on the nose, which referred to a railtour that had taken place in September 1996. The majority of the fifty 58s were exported or hired to other European countries, though a handful were cut up. This one was repatriated in 2006 and is shown as stored. (Paul Webber)

Summer 2001 and the Saturday only (SO) 13.03 departure from Paignton pauses at Torre with a Virgin CrossCountry set, including a DVT and an unidentified Class 47 in Virgin livery. (Martin Duff)

A Class 142 waits for the 'right away' from Torre Station with a train for Exeter on an unknown date *c.* 1987. Semaphore signals are still in use from the Grade II listed signalbox on the Up platform. (Author's Collection)

On Thursday 18 April 2002, 47818 (D1917) *Strathclyde* passes Powderham with the 09.13 Virgin Trains 1V45 Liverpool to Plymouth express. The loco is shown as still extant and last shown with DRS. (Author's Collection)

Transrail-liveried 37153 (D6853) with the 1Z10 08.00 Rhymney to Paignton railtour on 25 July 1999. It is seen here approaching Dawlish Station just after midday. The English Electric loco was built in July 1963 and was withdrawn five months after this railtour. It was subsequently cut up by Booths of Rotherham in January 2003. (Paul Webber)

On 13 December 1970 we see 46013 (D150) leaving Exeter St David's Station with an Up northbound train. An excellent study in infrastructure as it was almost fifty years ago. The Derby-built 'Peak' dates from December 1961. It was withdrawn in July 1980 and cut up in Swindon in April 1985. (Maurice Dart)

The unusual livery carried by 47829 (D1964) is seen here at Totnes with the 11.50 Plymouth to Liverpool train on Tuesday 26 March 2002. Last shown as stored at Long Marston and up for sale. (Author's Collection)

North British diesel hydraulic Class 22 D6307, seen here traversing the Down line at Mutley with a mixed freight train on 3 April 1970. Built in October 1959, it was withdrawn five months after this picture was taken and scrapped at Swindon later that year. (Maurice Dart)

On a summer Saturday morning in 2001 an infrequent scrap train from Exeter Alphington Branch is hauled by 60059 *Swinden Dalesman*. It was built at Brush Works in May 1991 but was stored until September that year. It is last shown as stored again in November 2010. (Martin Duff)

Great Western's 47815 (D1748/47155/47660) working down the sea wall at 17.29 on 27 July 1999. It was named *Abertawe Landore* a year later and then *Great Western* from 2005. It is still in service, last shown with Riviera Trains, Crewe. (Paul Webber)

47654 *Finsbury Park* piloting 47656 out of Newton Abbot on 20 June 1989. The service was the 1M09 08.47 Plymouth to Liverpool. Both 47s were manned and working. 47654 (D1640) was withdrawn in June 2002 and scrapped five years later, and 47656 (D1719) was withdrawn in January 2008 and is shown as stored. (Paul Webber)

Dawlish Warren on 7 March 1980 and 47519 (D1102) heads west with a train of Mk 1 and 2 coaches. Aside from being in the non-sequenced batch of numbers which were added towards the end of production, they were just like any other 47 built at Crewe. They were built in September 1966, withdrawn in February 1999 and cut up in October 2005. (Author's Collection)

Plymouth Station on 30 June 1988 and Network SouthEast-liveried 50032 *Courageous* is seen with a little over two years of service left. It was cut up at Old Oak Common in March 1991. (Maurice Dart)

This Class 22 North British diesel hydraulic D6318 is seen on Laira Depot on 7 April 1971. It was technically stored unserviceable (U), being withdrawn one month later and cut up at Swindon in March 1972. (Maurice Dart)

Early April 1994 at Calstock, two Class 37s top and tail on a Sunday railtour. (Martin Duff)

Dawlish Warren on Saturday 24 July 1999 and 6B68 is the 09.40 Burngullow to Alexandra Dock with Transrail-liveried 60063 *James Murray*. (Graham Bowden)

Brush 31128 (D5546) at Dawlish Warren on 3 July 1979. Built in August 1959, it served for forty years and is preserved (last shown with North York Moors Railway). (Paul Webber Collection)

November 2000 at Exeter St David's Station. During poor weather and loss of infrastructure this Class 47-hauled service started from Exeter. 47810 (D1924/47247/47655) *Porterbrook* was built in January 1966 and is still in service with DRS. (Martin Duff)

No book on Devon would be complete without a picture of one of the best longer distance units built since the first generation DMUs. 159001 is the first of the batch of twenty-two, three-car sets built at Derby in 1992/3, and is seen here at Plymouth on 11 September 2006. Ostensibly for use by South West Trains it is now used by South Western Railway for the Waterloo to South West of England Route. (Maurice Dart)

A picture taken in January 1989 shows an unidentified Network SouthEast liveried Class 50 passing through Dawlish Station in the Down direction over the Up line. The bi-directional signalling was used primarily for emergencies and engineering work, until recent years when it was cleared for use in regulating trains. (Author's Collection)

A rake of Mk 1 coaches and 37233 (D6933) are seen approaching Dawlish Station on Tuesday 28 August 1984. This was identified as the 1Z19 17.15 Paignton to Birmingham relief. (Paul Webber Collection)

Hymek D7018 and Warship 815 *Druid* with Warship 831 *Monarch* on the Up Main in the background. 11.00 ex-London Waterloo, running ninety-five minutes late, at Exeter St David's on Saturday 17 April 1971. A rare combination even for those days. D7018 survives on the West Somerset Railway. The Warship was withdrawn six months later and scrapped at Swindon in October 1972. 831 was similarly treated. (Maurice Dart)

An Exeter to Paignton stopper with 31309 at Dawlish in 1984. Built in May 1962, it was withdrawn twenty-eight years later and cut up in April 1992. (Paul Webber Collection)

EWS-liveried 'Tractor' 37695 had turned up at Dawlish earlier in the afternoon of 7 August 1999 hauling the 1V41 Liverpool to Paignton service, which it had taken on at Crewe, with 47851 ignominiously being dragged along on the tail end. Having run around at Paignton, the ensemble headed back north as 1M25 Paignton to Manchester, leaving Dawlish at 16.53. A total of nearly 440 miles were racked up for the day's work. The 47 looks to be ticking over at least, probably to provide for the train ETH system. (Paul Webber)

Operated by Fragonset at the time, green-liveried 47488 (D1713) was on hire to Virgin CrossCountry and hauling the 1M25 service off of Paignton. The consist was a Virgin DVT set. Pictured at Dawlish Warren at 16.54 on Saturday 10 June 2000, it is shown as still in existence but stored. (Paul Webber)

Still with eleven years of service in front of her, 31124 (D5542) is seen on an Up parcels service at Langstone Rock in June 1979. The angle of the sun suggests it is fairly early in the day so possibly returning newspaper vans. (Paul Webber Collection)

An undated photograph from early summer 2001 depicts the track recording unit stabled in Exeter Hyde Park siding. Rebuilt from a former Class 101 unit as a mobile laboratory, it is now preserved. (Martin Duff)

A bit of a celebrity loco in the sense that 50050 *Fearless* started life as D400, the very first Class 50 built and introduced in October 1967 on lease from English Electric. EE had built it in early 1966 using experience gained from experimental loco DP2, the Deltic lookalike. Here it is seen on Saturday 7 August 1982 at Newton Abbot West on the 'Motorail' train. (Author's Collection)

Exmouth Junction on Friday 25 September 1998 and 37505 (D6728) *British Steel Workington* and 37677 (D6821) depart with 7Z96, an Exmouth Junction to Westbury working. Both locos are no longer with us. (Graham Bowden)

Another unusual combination is seen passing through Dawlish on 30 August 1984: 31286 (D5818) with 50045 (D445) *Achilles* and two clay wagons in tow. This is possibly a trip freight from Heathfield. Neither loco are still with us, but the 31 was withdrawn in December 1991 and sold to the Bodmin & Wenford Railway. It was then resold back to BR and eventually cut up in December 2001. (Paul Webber Collection)

(D)1033 *Western Trooper* passing Starcross Yacht Club in the murk at Powderham on 14 July 1976. This was suggested to be the Up 'Clayliner' to the Potteries. The loco was withdrawn just a few weeks after this picture was taken but survived as a Steam Heating Unit for a further three years. It was cut up in May 1979 in Swindon Works. (Paul Webber Collection)

The locos stored at Meldon Quarry almost seemed forgotten they were there so long. 73103 (E6009) on 3 September 2004 in company with others, including 31301 (D5834). The 73 is shown as still in use, but now as 73970. The 31 was cut up in February 2011 by Booths of Rotherham. (Maurice Dart)

'Cromptons'
6573 (33055) and
D6571 (33053) on
a Special Charter
at Royal Albert
Bridge signalbox
on Monday
30 March 1970.
Double track right
up to the bridge, a
working signalbox
and semaphore
signals complete
this period picture.
The signalbox
survives as an office
for the duty MOM,
when covering
the Plymouth
district. D6571 also
survived and is
shown as privately
owned on the Mid
Hants Railway.
33055 was cut up
in August 1991.
(Maurice Dart)

The Up Limited
at Mutley with
D1027 *Western
Lancer* on Thursday
18 June 1964.
The 84A (Laira)
engine was around
five months old
at the date it is
seen here. It only
served for eleven
years; a tragic
waste of resources
and public money.
(Maurice Dart)

The 6B68 Burngullow to Alexandra Dock junction 'Silver Bullets' was in the hands of 37668 and 37680. They are seen passing Dawlish on Wednesday 28 July 1999. 37668 (D6957) had been allocated to St Blazey china clay traffic in 1994 and survives with West Coast Railway, Carnforth. 37680 (D6924) had been associated with Great Rocks aggregate traffic but found itself available for system wide use in this year. It was cut up in January 2011. (Paul Webber)

Approaching Sprey Point on the Teignmouth sea wall, on Saturday 24 June 1989, is 31465 and 31405 on 1M37 08.40 Paignton to Manchester. They would have worked down on the 2340 (F) Liverpool to Paignton, having come on at Birmingham. (Paul Webber)

In August 2001 RES-liveried 47727 (D1629) *Duke of Edinburgh's Award* waits to leave Minehead with an excursion for London. It is still operational with Colas Rail. (Martin Duff)

On Friday 15 May 1998 an immaculate 50031 *Hood* with a Plymouth to Paddington Special made up of Mk 1 stock. (Graham Bowden)

Newton Abbot and 47597 (D1597) on 1A01, a Plymouth to London Paddington Parcels train, is shown on Monday 20 May 1991. It was cut up in 2008, having been withdrawn one month earlier, after becoming a RES loco between October 1991 and February 2003. (Author's Collection)

Early 2002 and a Serco test train is seen from high up on Langstone Rock, rounding the curve toward Dawlish Warren. Or is it? Evidence suggests this train is travelling westwards (Down over the Up Reversible) as there is a loco on the other end and a tail lamp on the (what would be) rear loco! The Down signal is off and the reversible is on. (Martin Duff)

A cracking photo of sixteen-month-old Hymek D7068 at Mutley, with Southern Region empty coaching stock (ECS) to Plymouth Friary on Saturday 13 June 1964. Another scandalous waste of tax-payers' money. Less than nine years later it was withdrawn (December 1972), without receiving an overhaul, taken to Swindon and cut up in April 1975. (Maurice Dart)

On Friday 8 February 2002 a Derby to Paignton service is seen approaching Starcross with an unidentified Virgin Class 47 and a rake of Virgin Mk 2 stock. (Martin Duff)

Inside Laira HST Depot, on Saturday 10 November 1990, we find 50032 *Courageous*, 50035 *Ark Royal* and 50041 *Bulwark* whilst on a RCTS visit. 50035 had been withdrawn the previous month, and was cut up four months later at Old Oak Common. 50035 survives with 'The Fifty Fund' at the Severn Valley Railway (SVR), and 50041 had been withdrawn seven months earlier and was taken to Old Oak Common and cut up in July 1991. (Maurice Dart)

Barnstaple on 18 July 1997 and 33008 (D6508) *Eastleigh* arrives with the 15.48 service from Exeter St David's. The loco survives in preservation on 'The Battlefield Line'. (Graham Bowden)

On Saturday 29 September 2001 and the final loco-hauled working of the summer season reaches Paignton in the early evening. At the time it was largely expected to be the last train so scheduled before 'Voyagers' took over on the duty. However, this was delayed and loco haulage returned in 2002. The last weekend with full diagramming for Class 47s was 29 June 2002, with HST's and Voyagers gradually creeping in from the following weekend. It was late summer before the late afternoon service to Manchester succumbed, which itself carried on even after the apparent CrossCountry loco farewell on 19 August 2002. (Martin Duff)

Another picture from 29 September 2001, this time depicting the last summer Saturday of loco hauled, with the 08.58, a mixed livery set of Mk 2 stock, ready to leave Paignton. (Martin Duff)

Plymouth Station and 57602 (D1818/47337) *Restormel Castle* is in the sidings adjacent to Platform 8 on Saturday 30 July 2005. Of course, 57602 is still in service with First Great Western and regularly appears on the 'Night Riviera' sleeper service. Somewhat ironically, it is now back in (First-GWR) green livery in 2019. (Maurice Dart)

Exeter St David's Station and Network SouthEast-liveried 50028 (D428) *Tiger* is probably performing a run-round move off a Down Waterloo train, ready for the return journey, *c.* 1990. It was withdrawn in January 1991 and cut up at Old Oak Common the following July. (Author's Collection)

Summer 2001 and the Down daytime Motor Rail service from Paddington passes Aller on its way to Penzance. (Martin Duff)

Network SouthEast-liveried Class 50 50018 (D418) *Resolution* is seen passing along the estuary towards Plymouth with a similarly liveried train in June 1991 and just a couple of weeks left in service. It met its end eighteen months later at MC Processors, Glasgow. (Author's Collection)

June 2006 and an excursion to Kingswear with Fragonset Railways 47703 (D1960/47514) *Hermes* pulling a train of mixed Mk 1 and 2 coaches. The loco was withdrawn the following year and sold into preservation on the Wensleydale Railway. (Martin Duff)

A great picture capturing both the large logo era and the era of 'proper trains' so greatly missed today. Here 50019 (D419) *Ramillies* and 50043 (D443) *Eagle* are seen at Plymouth on Friday 21 September 1984. 19 survived into preservation and initially so did 43, but this was cut up in 2002. (Maurice Dart)

August 2001 on a summer Saturday at Aller. An unidentified Virgin Class 47 and ten matching Virgin coaches leave the branch with the 13.03 from Paignton. (Martin Duff)

An unidentified Virgin Class 47 leaves Dawlish Station on a wet summer Friday in 2001 with a Derby to Plymouth train. It consists of a mixed-liveried set of Mk 2 coaches. (Martin Duff)

Dawlish Warren on Saturday 24 July 1999. 1V35, the 06.20 Derby to Paignton service, with 47888 (D1713) in a recreated original livery. Withdrawn four years later, it is currently shown as stored. (Graham Bowden)

Another picture at Dawlish Warren on 24 July 1999, this time with 1E33 the 10.01 Paignton to Newcastle mail/parcels service with RES 47840 (D1661) *North Star*. Withdrawn in 2007, it survives in preservation on the West Somerset Railway. (Graham Bowden)

Virgin 47854 (D1972) *Women's Royal Voluntary Service* leaves Teignmouth with a Preston to Paignton service on Saturday 23 June 2001. This working regularly involved Mk 3 stock. Shown as still in service with the West Coast Railway Company. (Martin Duff)

On Friday 9 June 1989 we see 47369 (D1888) passing along the sea wall at Dawlish with a Heathfield empty stock working. It was withdrawn seven years later and broken up two years after that. (Graham Bowden)

An unidentified Network SouthEast Class 50 passes Aller, *c.* 1990, with a mixed set of Mk 1 and 2 coaches. (Author's Collection)

EWS Class 60 60006 *Scunthorpe Ironmaster* heading the 6V70 freight through Dawlish Warren on the evening of Friday 16 June 2000. (Paul Webber)

The first of thirty Class 67s, 67001 *Night Mail* is seen at Plymouth in company with a classmate, when just two years old, on Tuesday 12 March 2002. They usually worked in pairs on the Royal Mail/Post Office trains as an insurance policy in case of breakdowns. (Maurice Dart)

On 12 May 1999, at Exmouth Junction, we see 7W85, consisting of eight Sealions for an Exeter Riverside to Chard Ballast Drop, hauled by Transrail-liveried 37693 (D6910). Seven weeks later, this loco was hired by SNCF until 19 August 2000, when it was repatriated and put in store until it was cut up in May 2011. (Graham Bowden)

Not a sight we are ever likely to see again, a quadruple-headed train, and all four locomotives are unrefurbished examples. This is Crediton on Tuesday 4 January 1994 and a most unusual combination of four Class 37s: 37263 (D6891), 37191 (D6891), 37038 (D6738) and 37254 (D6954). In order these locomotives were: Withdrawn in March 2000 and preserved on Dean Forest Railway; withdrawn in January 2000 and stored at EWS (CRDC), Wigan; still operational with DRS; and withdrawn in January 1999 and preserved on Spa Valley Railway. (Graham Bowden)

Class 52 (D)1043 *Western Duke* ascending Torre Bank in the gloom on 16 July 1975. It is working 1A85, the 17.10 Paignton to Paddington. (Paul Webber Collection)

Four-month-old 66002 is seen here at Plymouth on 11 August 1999. One of several 66s and other locos drafted in for the Total Eclipse of the Sun special trains. The eclipse was a bit of a non-event in that it was almost invisible due to cloud cover, apart from it going dark, of course. That is aside from the hundreds of thousands of litres of bottled water stored in St Blazey Yard, the supposed gridlock on Cornwall's roads, and water and accommodation shortages, none of which occurred. As I held a motorcycle licence, I was given a course in advanced riding prior to the day. A motorcycle was hired for me for a couple of weeks so that I could respond to incidents and get through the traffic! (Maurice Dart)

Crediton on 18 March 2004 and a brace of Fragonset 33s. 33103 (D6514) *Swordfish* and 33202 (D6587) *Meteor* with the 5Z59 10.16 Westbury to Okehampton ECS move for the Dartmoor Railway. Both are preserved with D6514 working on the Swanage Railway. (Graham Bowden)

A First Transpennine-liveried 158766 at Umberleigh Level Crossing on Saturday 22 September 2007. Whether this was a permanent allocation to the South West or whether it was on temporary loan from the North of England is not known. (Maurice Dart)

Dawlish Station and 31257 (D5685) on 2C57, the 19.35 Exeter to Paignton, on 4 August 1977. It was withdrawn in September 1990 and cut up in April 1992 by Booths. (Paul Webber Collection)

Crediton on 14 August 1988 and 37372 (D6859) is with an Engineer's Train coming off the Okehampton Line. This loco is very interesting, as it was purchased for preservation after it was withdrawn in December 2004 and is kept at Barrow Hill, with a view to recreating a 'Baby Deltic' Class 23 loco using the 37 as a base. It shares many similarities to the (only) ten examples of the Class 23. The ten Class 23s lasted between nine and ten years, with one exception (in departmental use) lasting seventeen years. (Graham Bowden)

Dawlish Warren on Thursday 26 July 1990 and 47831 *Bolton Wanderer* is on an unknown working. It metamorphosised into 'Thunderbird' loco 57310 *Kyrano* in 2003. (Graham Bowden)

On Saturday 11 August 2001, 47815 *Abertawe Landore* crosses Cockwood Harbour with a Plymouth to Paddington mid-afternoon service. It is still operational with Riviera Trains, Crewe. (Martin Duff)

An unidentified Class 50 (possibly 50042) light engine passing through Newton St Cyres, probably heading to/from Meldon Quarry, *c.* 1989. (Author's Collection)

Warship (D)861 *Vigilant* at Boat Cove, Dawlish, heading 1B45, the 11.30 Paddington to Penzance, on Thursday 22 July 1971, on which day a partial solar eclipse also occurred. 861 was built in February 1962 and withdrawn in October 1971, being cut up nine months later at Swindon. (Ray Manning, Paul Webber Collection)

August bank holiday 2001 featured a Class 31 and an unidentified Class 33, both in Fragonset livery, seen here powering away from Dawlish with a Skegness to Paignton service. The 31 is 31602 (D5614) *Chimaera*, which is still operational with British American Railway. (Martin Duff)

A St Blazey to Exeter Riverside freight has 37229 and 37696 in charge as they pass the former Exminster signalbox on Monday 24 July 1995. By a quirk of fate these two – 37229 (D6929) and 37696 (D6928) – were actually twins. (Author's Collection)

Class 50 50031 *Hood* is seen here approaching Exeter St David's Station *c.* 1990. (Author's Collection)

The 09.13 1V45 Liverpool to Plymouth service, passing Powderham with 47843 *Vulcan* (the name was not carried between June 1989 and August 2000). As the name does not appear to be present, it dates the picture to between January 1997 and August 2000, when Virgin operated CrossCountry trains. The loco survives with Riviera Trains. (Graham Bowden)

A great picture of not only a lost locomotive and train, but of a lost infrastructure. Hymek D7027, at Bere Alston, on Monday 6 April 1964 with the 14.05 Plymouth to Waterloo. The loco was built in April 1962, withdrawn in November 1971 and subsequently stored (unserviceable) until it was cut up in Swindon nine months later. Fortunately, the route from Plymouth to Bere Alston survives, albeit as a single line, as does the connection to Gunnislake, seen curving off over the first coach. (Maurice Dart)

A rather grubby Network SouthEast-liveried 50032 (D432) *Courageous* at Newton St Cyres Station with 1Z18, the Taw-Retour to Barnstaple, on Sunday 16 September 1990. This was one of the final outings for 50032, being withdrawn the following month. (Author's Collection)

Waiting to leave Newton Abbot at 18.53 on Saturday 24 June 1989 were 31454 and 31460. They were working the 1M65 18.35 Paignton–Wolverhampton service. 31454 was still in existence until 2017, though its current status is unknown. 31460 was cut up in January 1997. (Paul Webber)

Another photograph of stored locos at Meldon Quarry. On Friday 3 September 2004 we see 47348 (D1829), 73117 (E6023) and 31301 (D5834). The 47 was cut up in January 2007, the 31 was cut up in February 2011, and the 73 survives, last shown at Barrow Hill. (Maurice Dart)

Passing Exminster with a Plymouth to Sheffield train is 47831 (D1618) *Bolton Wanderer* on Wednesday 26 July 1995. The loco went on to be rebuilt in 2003 as 57310 and survives on hire to Network Rail. (Author's Collection)

Cotswold Rail 47813 *John Peel* hauling a motley collection up through Cockwood in early evening on Sunday 9 July 2006. (Paul Webber)

HST 43160 and 43098 had set out from Edinburgh on the 07.10 Virgin CrossCountry service to Plymouth on 1 June 2002. By the time they had got to Exeter, assistance was mandated. This came in the form of 47733 *Eastern Star*. Clagging well, the ensemble is seen passing Langstone Rock at 16.55. Interesting to note that 43160 was involved in the collision at Plymouth on 3 April 2016, and on 14 September 2017 was damaged by fire at Exeter. (Paul Webber)

Large logo-liveried 50015 *Valiant* had headed down the Paignton branch light engine at 14.25 on 3 October 1990. Forty minutes later it reappeared with an HST set in tow. This was possibly the 1E37 14.25 Paignton to Newcastle service. Both power cars (43011 and 43194) were switched on. 43011 was involved in the Ladbroke Grove disaster and was subsequently cut up. (Paul Webber)

A rare combination of 58002 dragging 1V87, the 12.10 Liverpool to Penzance service, at Tiverton Junction on 1 September 1984. It was manned by a Saltley crew, who returned with the 58 light engine from Plymouth. (Paul Webber Collection)

HST (The Last Lap)

In 2019, we see the end of traditional HST operations in the West Country. No book about trains in Devon would be complete without a tribute to those wonderful and iconic machines that have traversed the 'Western' for over four decades. I have travelled on these hundreds of times, both as a passenger and in connection with my job, in particular when pilotworking them over various sections of Devon and Cornwall since 1992.

This HST photograph comes with no information whatsoever. I have included it as it epitomises everything we have come to love about these wonderful machines. They have traversed this stretch of line along the famous Devon sea wall between Starcross and Teignmouth for over forty years, both as the frequent service to Paddington from Cornwall and Devon, but also as a cross-country service to stations beyond Bristol. (Author's Collection)

Seen here departing Paignton on 29 September 2001 is this Virgin interregional HST for Edinburgh, with 43100 (254023) leading. (Martin Duff)

Rounding the curve on the Down approach to Teignmouth is 43196 (253057) with the 09.03 Paddington to Plymouth on Thursday 16 May 2019. (Martin Duff)

First Great Western (FGW) HST service from Paignton to Paddington in summer 2001. (Martin Duff)

A much-loved livery adorns 43176 (253047) at Exeter St David's Station on Saturday 8 February 1992. The train is the 09.35 Paddington to Plymouth service. (Author's Collection)

On Sunday 7 April 2019, the 08.05 Penzance to Paddington pauses at Totnes, 43018 (253009) leading. The footbridge had been renewed weeks before. The old one, which abutted the former signalbox, is due for reuse at Lostwithiel. (Martin Duff)

Plymouth Station sees 43088 (254017) on Friday 3 October 2008. (Maurice Dart)

Another Plymouth Station photograph sees 43009 (253004) on Friday 3 October 2008. (Maurice Dart)

In August 1992 an InterCity-liveried HST set was a familiar sight along the Devon coast. This unidentified set is probably a cross-country train returning north. (Author's Collection)

On Tuesday 25 March 2019, the 15.00 Plymouth to Paddington HST 'The Mayflower' heads across Exminster Marsh with 43185 (253052) leading. (Martin Duff)

On Saturday 6 April 2019 we can see the 11.56 Plymouth to Paddington service, with 43018 (253009) leading, shortly before departure for Paddington on a glorious Saturday lunchtime. (Martin Duff)

On Saturday 22 March 2019, 43078 (254012) calls at Exeter at 16.00 with 'The Mayflower'. Of note is the water bowser on Platform 4, provided for topping up HST coolant. (Martin Duff)

43185 *Great Western* pauses at Torquay with the 11.30 Paddington to Paignton service on Sunday 7 April 2019. This was a Sunday working that returned at 15.45. The signalbox closed in 1984. (Martin Duff)

Midland Mainline HST 43058 (254002) was on hire to Virgin at Plymouth on Thursday 12 October 2006. (Maurice Dart)

In Plymouth on 6 April 2019, 43018 leads the 10.00 service from Penzance to Paddington, whilst a CrossCountry HST set waits for its 12.25 departure time from Platform 8. (Martin Duff)

Again on 6 April 2019, 43187 (253053) is at the rear of the 09.18 Paignton to Paddington service. The Saturday working was formed by an ECS from Laira. (Martin Duff)

About to pass over Red Cow Crossing and into Exeter St David's Station on Saturday 16 July 1983, an unidentified HST is seen in the early livery. (Author's Collection)

On Tuesday 25 March 2019 at 13.31 in Exeter St David's, 43162 (254037) *Exeter Panel Signalbox* is seen at the front of 'The Mayflower' – the 11.03 Paddington to Plymouth service. 43185 was the rear power car. (Martin Duff)

HST 43043 (253021) is seen here on hire to Virgin Trains at Plymouth on 12 October 2006. (Maurice Dart)

On Sunday 7 April 2019 43196 (253057) was on the front of the 11.01 Penzance to Paddington, seen here at Newton Abbot. (Martin Duff)

On Thursday 27 March 2019 an unidentified CrossCountry HST is seen working the 15.25 Plymouth to Leeds across Exminster Marsh. (Martin Duff)

On Sunday 7 April 2019 HST 43018 was the lead power car on the 08.05 Penzance to Paddington, seen at Totnes. The footbridge had recently been renewed. (Martin Duff)

On 25 March 2019, 43185 *Great Western* leads 'The Mayflower' at Exminster Marsh. (Martin Duff)

On 22 March 2019 a slightly delayed 1V50 Edinburgh to Plymouth calls at Exeter St David's as 'The Mayflower' leaves for London Paddington at 16.02. In the Up direction is the rear power car, 43303 (43103/254024), of a CrossCountry service. (Martin Duff)

On 6 April 2019, 43171 (253045) was the lead power car on the 06.50 Penzance to Paddington service. It is captured here at the scheduled stop at Newton Abbot. (Martin Duff)

Saturday 6 April 2019 and 43187 (253053) was on the back of the 09.18 Paignton to Paddington service 'The Torbay Express'. 43198 (253058), the ultimate HST power car, is leading. (Martin Duff)

Tuesday 2 April 2019 and original liveried W43002 (253001) pauses at Exeter St David's at 09.57 with the 06.47 Penzance to Paddington service. This was the last time W43002 worked a full-length HST set before the final day of the fleet. (Martin Duff)

On Monday 27 March 2019, the 14.03 Paddington to Penzance service rushes across Exminster Marsh toward Starcross and the far west. The photographer used the bridge parapet, with its painted line reference and mileage, as the main framing for the picture. (Martin Duff)

On 25 March 2019 W43002 was on the rear of the 12.04 Penzance to Paddington service, which restarted at Plymouth. The HST was sent down from St Philips Marsh specially. It was routed via Platform 6 at Exeter St David's. (Martin Duff)

The last full-length HST to travel from Penzance to London Paddington in regular scheduled service was 1A78, on 18 May 2019. Having done thousands of miles on these wonderful locomotives over the years, in both an official capacity (usually as a pilotman) and as a passenger, I thought it only fitting to travel on the last one. So, I travelled from St Austell to Exeter St David's (in first class of course and in company of former colleagues, including Martin Duff) and took this photograph as it prepared to depart from Exeter for Paddington. 43093 (254019) *Old Oak Common HST Depot 1976–2018* led the train and 43188 (253053) *The Welshman* brought up the rear. (Author)

Acknowledgements

Thanks once again to my wife, Julie, for her support whilst compiling this, my seventh book. Thanks also to Connor Stait and the team at Amberley Publishing. All photographs are credited accordingly. Every effort has been taken to establish copyright where none is shown on original photographs and I apologise for any photographs incorrectly credited.

Content

Photographic content and additional notes supplied by G. Bowden, M. Dart, M. Duff, P. Webber and the author.

Reference Sources

www.brdatabase.info
The Complete UK Modern Traction Locomotive Directory by Colin J. Marsden (2011).
My own contemporaneous notes and archive records.